Poetries
Abstract Art – Poetry – Prose

Doug Rucker

Poetries
by Doug Rucker
Layout by Helane Freeman

Doug Rucker
Vilimapubco
Malibu, CA
ruckerdoug@gmail.com

For permission requests, sales to U.S. bookstores and wholesalers, or to inquire about quantity discounts, please contact the publisher at the email address above.

Library of Congress Control Number: 2021903868

ISBN 978-1-7354717- 3-0

First Edition
10 9 8 7 6 5 4 3 2 1

Printed in the United States of America

Contents

Introduction

I was reading a book describing art as a kind of visual poetry. This fascinated me because I like to participate in both art and poetry. In fact I've just completed a little book describing my feelings about abstract art and how they are similar to my feelings in response to poetry. The book you're reading is devoted one-third to illustrated abstract art.

The second third is of recent poems occurring to me at this point in my lifetime. As if I hadn't an ounce of control on what they'd be, I'm helpless about their content. I opened the doors of my imagination, and these weird thoughts fell out. If in the coming months I'm struck with another urge to poeticize, I have no guarantee what they'll be about. I'll just record them and put them down to *"history of the good and bad!"*

In the last third are poems are derived from prose already written. Besides what is said, the only difference between prose and poetry is the way it's placed on paper. Prose is written horizontally like the page of a book, while poetry is written vertically in shorter paragraphs with spaces between. The power that connects them is what they have to say. What they say may be boring and forgettable and *tough to convert*, or harmonious and poetically written and *easy to convert.*

The value of poetry is in what and how it's written and maybe not how it's put down. The creator is as good at whatever level he's reached.

Poetries

Abstract Art – Poetry – Prose

Weaving - On Abstract Art

It reminds me of weaving which
confirms my permission to give it
a name. Is it a close-up of cloth?

    Black, purple and green
    on all four sides make
    a remarkable frame
    surrounding the middle,
    and establishing its rank.

Green is the symbol of
growth! Black is the symbol
of power, allowing me to
believe the base at the bottom
is where everything begins.

    It is the source for brilliance
    as has been created above.

The black and the purple
on the left and the right
hold the center of interest
so it can't get away.

    Were the center of interest
    beginning to move,
    the black and the purple
    are diminished at top, so it
    would escape and upward

toward the sky, toward expression
and freedom. The oversized, blown-up
threads of gray and white are heavily
tinged with magenta and touches of
green that are borrowed from its source.

Gray and white, symbols of
purity, intellect and wisdom
involve magenta, the symbol
of universal love at its highest,

and showing the importance of
thick threads, symbolic of nobility
and wisdom, weaving and
feelings of power and strength.

Let us rejoice!

Weaving

What do you See? - Poetry

Frustration and turmoil.

How so?
Let me count the days.

How many are there?
A year is 365,
but I may live longer -
or shorter.

Have you liked it here?
Between the bad and the good
there is always the middle.

What's the bad?
Almost dying at 18 months,
divorce at a critical time.
Death of my first wife.
Death of my second wife.
Ongoing trials of my children.

What's the good?
My early upbringing.
My successes at high school.
My life as an athlete.
My first marriage and children.
My second marriage and her children.
My success as an architect.
My success as an artist.

My success as a writer.
My luck with a pacemaker and
outliving an average life span.

> *Sounds like you've had more*
> *good than bad.*

That's true.

> *Do you like the good things?*

Yes!

> *Do you hate the bad things?*

Yes!

> *Are you grateful for your life?*

Yes!

> *Would you change anything?*

Yes, but it's impossible.

> *Do you mind coming to the end?*

It depends on how.

> *How would you like?*

Alert and evolving
that suddenly ceases.

Skiing – From Prose

Last weekend a man from Mars
was shushing down a small slope
and falling whenever he lost balance,
then getting up and shushing again!

> You haven't heard? People from
> other planets have been visiting
> earth for quite some time now.
> Anyway, he was falling down again

and again all the way to the bottom.
Skiing straight down the slope was all
he could do. My friend urged him to
go up the hill twice as high and then try

> traversing down the slope. He did as suggested,
> and while he traversed in one direction he
> turned and tried to traverse in the other
> direction, but he couldn't make it all the way

around and gravity took over his shushing
inaptness and he found himself again hurtling
straight down the slope, trees flashing,
skis bouncing, snow swirling in a blur as

> he hurtled out of control, down the
> slope. The wind whistled in his hair
> and cooled his legs through wet Levi's.
> Tears from the cold wind formed in his

eyes as he gained speed. He was helpless
with fright and didn't know how to
snowplow. Looming before him was a
long line of skier's waiting for the lift.
Skiers stretching 50 yards to the left and

      skiers stretching 50 yards to the
      right with a solid looking log-cabin
      clubhouse behind. He was not only
      to injure the innocent but also
      break a leg on the building.

He leaned desperately to the left
to try to turn himself parallel
to the line. At the last moment
both skis began to bite into the

      snow leaving a spray on the
      alarmed faces of those waiting for the
      ski lift. He traveled swiftly along the
      line, seeing each face zip by, *66, 67,*

68, etc. Eventually, he passed the crowd
and, because the snow began to rise,
came to a stop, glanced around rather
proudly, took a deep breath and fell down.

Blast from the Past - On Abstract Art

Notice the red and yellow ball
rocketing out of nowhere
invading an orange shape
that reminds me of a swastika.

The orange center is backed by
greenish boards with black intrusions
calling forth unintelligible days.

It is made to outdo itself
and go topsy-turvy
with a twist and a turn
and a number of flip-flops!

I shall forget where I am,
and who I am, and
why I'm here and let
my mind wander at will.

Perhaps this is a game board,
and by conjuring magic game balls
I can move them across a series
of imaginary crosses arranged
on a four-square board – *or not!*

There are sixteen crosses making
nine fine squares, and now suppose
two colored balls, the first yellow
and red, the second green and blue.

The first ball symbolizes Country A,
meaning Intelligence and Power.
The second ball symbolizes Country B
meaning Growth and Contentment.

As presidential players and leaders
of respective governments at war,
and with knowledge that for each
the conflict means destroying property

terrible unhappiness and wasting
lives. The loser will have to change
his country to symbolize the vibrant
power-banner of the winner.

Can either country A or B
accept only *Intelligence and Power*
or only *Growth and Contentment?*

Before the war, perhaps
each should agree to
embrace other and declare
peace by having both.

Blast from the Past

Lightning is My Name - Poetry

Way off in the distance
amidst darkening clouds
and a rumble and a grumble,
I flash a warning,
and maybe another.
When chips are down
and my anger is up
unreasoning embers
burn in my heart
giving naught to the devil
burst with a flash
and strike while it's hot!

Lightning is a Farce! - Poetry

Wham! Bam!
goes the lightning!
It really whacked off
a big one that time!
I was tipsy, anyway
and fell off my chair.
It was sudden, like,
no kidding!
like I tell you,
GaBoom! GaBoom!
Others were shocked, too,
though not enough to
have spilled their coffee.
So, you or me? Who's
the macho man here?

Lightning is Philosophic - Poetry

What do you think about lightning?
I think it's pretty cool,
that is, if it doesn't
strike you on top of the head
and onvert your skull
to a black cinder!
Aren't you being dramatic?
Truth is in between.
Grasping considers mostly good.
Aversion considers mostly bad.
Truth considers good and bad.
Lightning's in the middle?

Lightning is intellectual - Poetry

A flash of light!
Did you see that?
Yes, and now a sharp crack
with a wobbly rumble.
The flash of light
and the time between,
the crack and rumble
was much too short.
How many seconds between?
Give it three!
At eleven hundred feet per second
it's thirty-three hundred feet away?
How far is that to a Ne'er-do-Well?
Close enough to worry!

Santa Ana Wind - From Prose

One Saturday while no one was working,
I stopped to see the newly poured
Hauffe foundation. I also wanted to look
at the view and dream about the completed

> house; enjoy the day and construction
> of a job I took seriously. The Santa Ana
> wind from the northeast was howling
> down the hill. It had come blasting

across the hot desert sweeping up
one side of the Malibu Mountains
and swooping down the long, smooth
slope toward our new house and ocean.

> In surprisingly forceful gusts, the
> wind came leaping and bucking
> and blowing and growling. The ocean
> in the lee of the mountains was

like rippled purple glass, and the gale
was raising heavy chop beyond the
Point and out to sea. With disheveled
hair walking crosswind with fists

> shoved deep into sweatshirt pockets,
> I made my way leaning against the
> wind. If the wind had stopped,
> I'd have fallen on my face. But I

enjoyed it. The wind was fresh and
exhilarating. I felt alive, important and
meaningful. The wind proved I was an
essential planetary being in the world.

I counted! It reminded me of my
Chicago days where the forces of
wind and nature blew with the intensity
of life or death. I experienced the pure

affects of the Santana wind on my person
and the solid earth holding my foundation
that would secure my creation. I was ecstatic
and lived for that fleeting moment in the wind!

Jumble Box - On Abstract Art

It's a jumble all right!
The square black border
shows it's boxy!

> Orange and black and blue
> remind me of words like effective,
> commanding, authority.

There's a black exit just past shades
of brown and orange leading nowhere.

> Is nowhere the dimness of the mind
> or a black hole with wriggling snakes,
> or a darkened pool profound and deep
> with steam arising, then vanishing in the dark?

The mysterious blue might be
an enchanted pool and once immersed
your most ecstatic dreams might come true.

> Having just discovered
> my reason for being
> or my worst nightmare,

shall I plunge my hand into that black hole
and grasp whatever joy or horror
I find wriggling when it returns?

> Do I chance taking a dive into the pool
> and thrusting deep to see another world,
> one with setting sun and two moons rising?

In the foreground there's a sandy beach
and shoreline bursting with trees
whereupon three mermaids loving
and living in leisure, languorously lie.

When from the sinister ocean
a boil of water from something
big below breaks forth in frightening
form and plunges toward the
mermaids who scramble to
the sea and swim for their lives.

I accost the chilling monster and ask him,
"Why scare the mermaids?" The monster,
heavy lips and drooling hair, soulfully
looks at me and says, *"I wanted to enjoy*

their beauty." I say, "
You must be gentle."
He responds, *"I know."*

Volumes of black clouds descend
and threaten the surface of the water.

A lightning flash ignites the
waves, trees and sandy beach.
Its jagged lines rip my eyes.

It's time to return to intelligence and
the contented light of an odd day that
as I look, has nothing to do with a Jumble Box.

Jumble Box

The vitality of life - Poetry

My brain is what I do.
My soul is who I am.
I cannot do what I do
without being who I am.
I'm stuck with that,
and can't get off!

> In my living existence
> I embody the softness of curls
> that twist through my body
> and allow me to feel
> the passions of things
> and the terror of things.

I can do a variety of effects.
Come and go like a spider.
Come and go like a rabbit.
Come and go like a blue jay.

> Though on certain days,
> my soul is stressed, but
> my brain is contented.
> On other days
> my brain is stressed and
> my soul is also stressed.

At these times I'm
stuck with myself
and can't get off!

> It might be reasoned
> I can do what I want,
> and forget the soul.
> But the soul is a maxim
> and can't be forgotten.

The soul is made from
birth, childhood, adolescence,
marriage, family, children, the
meaning of life, then if lucky,
retirement, old age and death.
It will not be governed by the
desire or not, of a day or two.

      So, I'm forced to be what I am
      rather than having a choice about
      who I'd rather be and I must
      concede I am stuck with
      myself and can't get off.

The question is:
how can I be happy
with a disturbed soul?
Or if I have a disturbed
soul, must there always
be a disturbed happiness?

      Sometimes humans, for a time,
      forget what disturbs them,
      and are happy for a while,
      and somehow subsist.

Though I might wish it otherwise,
perhaps this is the answer.
I must accept these as facts
and must *"suck it up!"*

      The ultimate truth is
      I'm stuck with myself
      and can't get off.

Daydreams – From Prose

Some days with a pick and shovel
down by the telephone pole I
moved laterally along the hillside
to make pathways or *bunny trails*

>to negotiate the steeply sloping half-acre
>below. Watching carefully for poison
>oak and rattlesnakes, I worked the trails
>to a rocky edge that sloped more steeply
>into a ravine. At times, out of sight

under an overhanging sumac, I'd
sit down to rest, gather my wind
and dream about a future time when
I might build a guest house spanning

>the thirty-foot barranca. Mentally I'd
>work out a simple glass-enclosed
>living space across the deep gully
>with double-pitched roof and maybe

a skylight with a wide redwood
deck cantilevered dramatically
into space. It'd have a bath in the
back, space for an in-line kitchen,

>dining counter and maybe a small,
>sculpturally formed, contemporary
>metal fireplace, a Fire-Drum.
>*(I'd create beautiful harmony.)*

Lost in impractical dreams,
I'd eventually return to the house
for a peanut butter and banana
sandwich on fresh white bread

and a glass of cold milk with
maybe a cookie for desert.
Then I'd return for the afternoon
to complete the brushing and
have a few more daydreams.

The Picture and the Person - On Abstract Art

Count 'em! Count 'em! Count 'em!
There are only four colors.
Black, red, blue and light blue.

Black is power, strength and mystery.
Red means blood, fire and passion.
Blue implies depth, expertise and stability.
Light blue signifies peace, reliability & tranquility.

Though positioned with a sense of
rhythm and harmony, the shapes and
lines are all over the place and the
quantity of items is larger than normal.

Is this a picture of a person? Someone
made of these elements would be well-
balanced with the power of strength and
conviction behind his or her philosophy

as well as a passion for doing his or
her own life's work – whatever that is.
He or she would also be a person of
depth, expertise and stability who has

a character of trustworthiness and
reliability. In effect, if this picture
were a person, I think I'd like someone
with these basic characteristics.

In this picture, as for quantity of
action, the abstract composition
is almost everywhere at once and
dances through space and time

       The bottom line: To be everywhere
       at once equals awareness and
       universal clarity, something
       I'd love for my own kids.

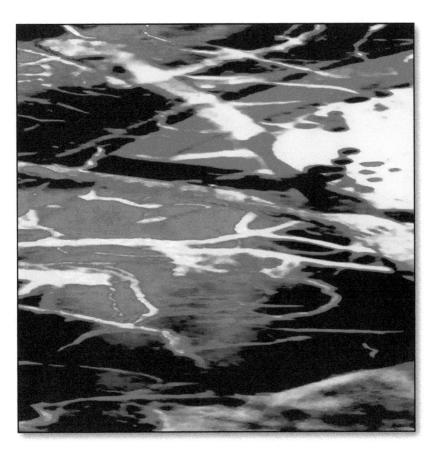

The Picture and the Person

Look Down and See - Poetry

A computer keyboard
designed to write
the story of my heart.

And of what is it filled?
Love and hate and in between.

What is it you love?
My story of love
for another I have loved.

And what is it you hate?
Pain, sickness and death.
Trials, troubles, tribulations.

Isn't it so with everybody?
It's the story of life,
adamant and true.

Can't it be otherwise?
It's written on the wind;
nobody changes the wind.

So, what are you to do?
Examining the truth,
diminishing the woe,
with energy of youth,
I go with the flow.

Surfing at Ventura – From Prose

On an overcast day with the wind
blowing in from a cold ocean I spent
a Ventura day surfing with Gene Grounds.
Gene would go zipping down a wave a
quarter mile away playing like a dolphin.

> I might as well have gone alone,
> for I only caught a glimpse of him
> now and then half disappearing
> beneath the back of a huge swell
> on its way to an explosion on sand.

The Ventura surf mounded up in long
lines before it pounded into the earth and
spilled on shoreline with a deafening roar!
The break had no relationship to the
perfect curls at Malibu's Surfrider Beach.
Brown, ugly, unforgiveable, the waves
towering like an overturning semi, tumbled
and broke to destroy everything in its path.

> My friend, Gene, who had ridden
> thirty-foot waves in Hawaii, managed
> to enter the water and paddle out
> beyond the break line. But me, at
> the top of the wave staring down into
> the yawning depths before me, I didn't
> know whether to go left, go right, or
> freeze like the anxious coward I am.

Sometimes I paddled up a mountainous
breaker, the tip of the board and me looking
straight up at the overcast sky, the crest of the

wave in crisis dribbling wildly at the top ready
for the fall. Waves broke at ungodly heights
and then would collapse on me like a waterfall.

> Underwater, I'd spin in the black depths
> and often felt I'd die. Board, torn from
> my grasp, bouncing and splashing to shore
> like a deer escaping a lion, I'd find myself
> tumbling alone holding my breath in the
> murky depths of the brown salt water.

With hair swirling, surf roaring in my ears
and water up my nose, I struggled upward to
reach muddy foam. It was like being tumbled
in a washer and trying to keep my head. I was
in a quandary as to which way was up! I'd stay
spinning until the wave flattened my body and
when it weakened, my body began stabilizing.

> Eyes barely opened in slits without
> breathing, I'd notice which way the
> body wanted to float. Full of air, the
> body always floats Up. Up to thick
> moist air and popping, fizzing foam.
> I never caught a wave, but on the
> bright side of things, I didn't die!

That day, the personality of the Ventura
break was perilous, erratic, unpredictable,
and relentless. I tested my courage, won
out to some degree and had a passable time.
For what it's worth, I gained experience
and looking back I guess I had no regrets.
Gene had a great time!

The Message - On Abstract Art

Seeing a piece of abstract
art chosen at random,
what could the message be?

I'll admit there's a certain
decisiveness about the picture.

The strong black lines are
determined to get through.

They contain a message.
but from where
and to whom?

From outer space?
From the room next door?
From the whisper of a tree fairy?

Or maybe telepathic information
from the recently dead?
Perhaps this is just a picture
of *"passing through."*

The black strip on the left
can be visualized as
the darkness and the blackness
of impenetrable night
through which it would be
 miraculous for anyone to pass.

Or what about the marching
 black bands shown distinct
and beautifully designed
with the urgency of life
and power to travel straight
to the unknown?

The message might be
the earth is the vehicle
upon which we ride
in our orbit around the sun

 in the company of
 eight different planets
 in a galaxy of 100 billion
 stars with the possibility

of dark matter
and dark energy
controlling our positions
and keeping our world

VIABLE.

The Message

Dream Poem with Lightning - Dream

It's a rainy, dream-gray evening
in a low wooden house with lots
of glass in the windows under a
deep cloud. Outside gets darker.

       Rain builds to a violent storm.
       I call Marge from the other room
       and meet her at the entry made
       of two glass doors and a skylight.

Through each door
I see lightning flashes
and hear thunderclaps
as two lightning bolts
strike the ground,
smack, crack, each
side of the house.

Poem Continues

It's still dream-gray. I'm alone
on the end of a pier. Waves
are billowing in the distance.

       A particularly large one
       is mounding in a long line.
       Its force will test the pier.
       I watch with morbid interest.

The rising tide provokes
the surge. I decide to return
to shore looking landward
down the narrowing pier
that's high above the water
on the seaward side, but
submerged toward shore
where I'd be forced to cross;
where waves have crashed in
volumes of swirling water and
have buried the top of the pier

But the wave rushes out
leaving wet sand.

I leap and run to shore.

Walking the Beams – From Prose

Now I'm not a steel man, but I have
seen pictures of steel workers calmly
walking tall and upright along the tops
of steel beams perhaps fifty or sixty
stories above the miniscule roofs of

New York City. I was impressed! How
could they be so casual? A missed step
and they'd fall screaming to their deaths.
Seeing a steel worker atop a super-
structure is like plummeting Niagara

Falls in a barrel, or bungee jumping
the Golden Gate, or flying below the
rim of the Grand Canyon. Scary but
fun? I wanted to walk my own beams.
One Saturday morning while visiting

the job alone, I gathered my courage
and climbed a ladder from the motor
court level to the top of the
cantilevered structure. Giving up
actually walking the beams, I sat down

with my feet on either side of
the lower flange straddling the
highest southeast beam, the one
thrusting boldly toward Palos
Verdes. I grabbed the top flange

with my fingers, or should I say
knuckles that were certainly white,
and inched my way forward moving
out on this farthest most protruding beam.
Unfortunately, as you may remember,

though the beam tops were level,
the beam bottoms were tapered.
Beginning at twenty-four inches
deep, they terminated at eight
inches deep. As I approached

the end I could no longer brace
myself as solidly with my feet.
I was tippy. Halfway out with
nothing under me but thrilling
spasms, shivers, and death,

I decided to stop. At thirty-five
feet above the earth, though
it looked a hundred and thirty-five,
the view was good enough.
There was nothing out there

but the horizon, a vast expanse
of ocean, Palos Verdes and me, with
tousled hair and white knuckles.
I didn't feel so badly about stopping
halfway out. After all, I wasn't a steel worker.

Explosion - On Abstract Art

It doesn't suggest a mountain,
or a building, or a person,
but resembles an explosion!

Where is the explosion?
In outer space!

Why's that?
I see tiny portions
of blue-black strips as frigid
quantities of infinite space.

*We both know you did not go
into outer space and snap
something colliding
with something else.*
"Mea culpa! I admit, an
explosion in outer space is
an out and out prevarication."

*The center of the detonation
is the point of the formidable
dark blue from which
everything discharged.*
Yes! The position from which
everything moved is well designated.

From there, widening ridges
of brilliant fiery orange
traveling at immense speeds
are rapidly expanding
and gradually cooling
to a royal red-purple.
What blew up?
Mankind's final solution
by interplanetary travel
to save itself;
a huge spacecraft
a hundred yards long
and fifty yards wide
carrying a thousand humans
twelve light-years distant
to EXO-Planet *4158*
 called ***Paradisium.***

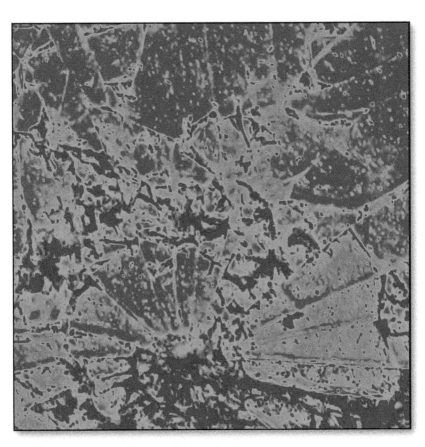

Explosion

I Am a Pool Table - Poetry

I am a pool table.

Here we go again.
"Figuratively speaking," that is,
I am a pool table.

Tell me about it.
Actually, I'm an *outdoor* pool table.
If I were this specific pool table I might
be thinking the following thoughts:

Pool tables don't think.
I'm outside under a huge canvas covering
supported by steel pipes ten feet apart.
There are no walls and wind blows through.

On the north side are windswept trees and
mowed lawns in a calm, park-like setting.

On the south side are buildings close by
providing moderate shade on a hot summer day.

On the east and west, the park nuzzles into
a quiet residential neighborhood accustomed to
"peace on earth, good will toward men."

In my long-term, sturdily built presence,
I sit, day in and day out, but also night in
and night out, and if you'll pardon the
expression, my fifteen balls are:

either chaotically at rest on the table,
or in the corner and mid-table pockets,
or aimlessly thrown over hard-packed
ground of decomposed granite, including
the eight ball under the table epitomizing
the caretaker of the pool table, if any.

No one loves the fun game of pool.
No one delights in the game of snooker.
No one cares for a skilled game of billiards
No one takes care of the pool table.

Occasionally, coming back from a walk
in the park, a friend might pick up a ball
or two and throw it either on the table
or off the table. My triangular ball-rack
is usually found ignored and forgotten
under an outdoor chair, or carelessly
thrown on the ground into a far corner.

Who plays pool outdoors in an outdoor tent?
Those who don't frequent pool halls?
Those who know nothing of an age-old tradition?
Those who don't question the need for an
indoor game table in an outdoor location?

Players are lucky if the pool table is level.
Imagine setting the cue ball down on
the flat, green velvet for a shot and it
slowly begins to roll. You have to prop
the legs with a stone to begin the game.

But, *"Now the day is over. Night is drawing nigh."*
Balls are in their pockets or in disarray on the
ground, or some under an outdoor chair lost
in the corner of the tent. The sticks are carelessly
thrown on the ground, or crisscrossed on the tabletop.

> Twilight is settling in, and as daytime ends the
> temperature becomes disturbingly low. I am a
> heavy table and rest on animal-shaped wooden
> legs that wiggle down to stop in catlike claws that
> clasp round, white balls upon which sit the lux-
> urious form of my once-sophisticated pool table.

It's 2:00 AM and the 3/4 moon high in the night sky
is casting blue-black shadows from the trees and breeding
black holes in the landscape from questionably solid
forms. I rest with on my planet in an unearthly quiet and
it's a time for dreaming and acknowledgment of
anything incredible arising from troubled thoughts.

> Jupiter and Mars are two feet apart in a duet for
> the pleasure of nocturnal creatures. Rising myster-
> iously in the east is Venus, casting loving rays upon
> the earth, inspiring every living creature to a good
> life on this planet for every miniscule stay.

Do I like my non-existent life as a pool table?
Good and bad are always inseparable! If I've lost
an eye, I've got another one. If I've lost a leg,
I've got another one. If I've lost everything, I still
have life and where there's life, there's hope.

Angry Neighbor – From Prose

At 9:30 AM, Mrs. Smith, in curlers,
housecoat and worn slippers, marched
out of her house and with hands on hips
stood defiantly in front of us and demanded,
"Well?! What are you up to now?!"

Since I always treated people politely,
I quietly replied, *"I'm seeing about a
loan for a house."* She said she didn't
like it. The property was too steep. The
traffic and noise would disrupt her family.

The neighborhood didn't want a house
down there. Building on that steep site
was insane and ridiculous. If God were
watching on that bright early morning
he'd have seen three people standing

alone in the middle of the street near the
cul-de-sac. A belligerent woman head
thrust forward in a confrontational pose,
questioning an architect in jeans and T-shirt
accompanied by a well-dressed banker

in a fresh suit jacket attempting to
grasp what was happening. *"Jim, here,
is going to lend me the money."* I said.
Mrs. Smith glowered at Jim and
demanded, *"Well, are you?"*

Jim ever so slightly rocked on his heels
while the question hung in the air.
Jim felt more or less insulted with the
effrontery and the unanticipated rudeness
of the women in curlers. He disliked

the callousness and self-absorption
of my angry neighbor. Then, after
hesitating a moment and looking her in the
eye, said softly and convincingly, *"Yes!"*

Mrs. Smith did an about face and stalked
back to her house. Jim and I watched her.
Jim had not listened to his head, but had
replied from his sense of inner justice.
He was compelled to reply, *"Yes."*

If Mrs. Smith had not been so disagreeable,
chances were six-to-one Jim would have
answered, *"No."* I got the loan because
Jim was ticked-off with our neighbor.
The Lord works in mysterious ways.

I can imagine a conversation:
"How did you get the loan?"
"From our angry neighbor."

See the Birdie – On Abstract Art

Speaking in general,
and since I know no other
way to speak right now,
still, I have something
important to impart.

I'm not sure what it is, but
I feel it will be justified when
out in the open and plain
for me and everyone to see.

It will be for people to think upon,
comment upon, criticize or offer
suggestions of their own. I take my
cue from abstract pictures I've drawn
to understand my subconscious mind.

Certainly, pictures drawn without
thinking come from a place empty
of any logical consideration. They
would be poems originating from
a natural place devoid of logic, but
composed like dreams with thoughts,
reasons, actions, loves, fears and
all the feelings and implications of
life on earth since the beginning of time.

Let's try one. I called this one
See the Birdie. Red catches the eye
and according to the rules, colors first!
The power of red equals the sun,
fire and passion. In this picture,
it grabs the eye as if a mother's child.

       Life and nature can't give up red
       no matter what! The background,
       green is predominant, as well, and
       claims the power of foliage and growth.
       An oval of contentment is blue and
       compelled to save face. It adopts the
       key spot dead center of the picture.

The darker green is more restful and
encourages the rest of the picture to
maintain a healing nature and *"consideration
for others."* Since the dominant three shapes
are fatter ovals rather than thinner ovals,
the picture suggests fullness and health,
rather than starvation and emptiness.

       This shows us the picture is happier
       rather than hollow and unhappy.
       The protocol next requires we look
       at the quantity of elements in the art.
       Since there are only three such forms
       telling us the picture's story, we must agree
       the picture is simpler than more difficult.

That leaves the question, what does the
abstract picture mean? What is the
unconscious mind telling us about
its physical, permanently attached body?
There is no one closer to myself than
my unconscious mind and if I don't
know that, what am I missing?

    Since the unconscious mind only informs
    me of my feelings, it leaves my logical
    interpretations and translations solely
    to an unaccomplished me with my lack
    of aptitude for telling expressions.
    To quote my literary friend, T. S. Eliot,
    "Let us go then, you and I, when the
    evening is spread out against the sky . . . "

This person *(me)* is extremely sensitive
to the sun and the powers and passions,
not only of life and all its ramifications,
but also the colors of life, especially red.
He also senses strong caring and feels the
love a mother has for her child.

    This is reinforced by a regard for growing
    nature in the color of green, including
    a bluish tint in the strong horizon just before
    sunset in a powerful ocean. The oval of blue
    shows he's *(I'm)* contented and basically at
    peace with the world.

Fatter rather than thinner suggests he has
a sense of health. He's eaten well and is
no longer hungry, therefore, not in despair.
These comments relate to the feelings of the
picture. And since the abstract art only tells us
of feelings rather than logic, we have our answer.

The answer to what does the abstract
picture mean is basically a positive
feeling of a person sensitive to the
energy of the sun and its powers and
passions plus the colors of life. He loves
green-growing things, therefore the
ongoing energy of life and love.

In this abstract picture, he tells us he is
basically contented with life on earth,
and loves fullness rather than emptiness. He
indicates he is well fed and at peace with
the world. Humorously, he invites we of the
earth's population to relax and *See the Birdie!*

See the Birdie

I'm a Lonely Star – Poetry

On some nights
rarely to be seen,
I'm a lonely star.
I come and go as
if in a dream.
Perhaps I am a dream.

At twilight or on a misty night,
I'm so far away I cannot be found
and I question my own existence.
Perhaps, I've dreamed myself.

But on rare nights, I've heard reports
my weakened light can be detected
though dimly, quietly and faintly, high
in some lost part of the cool night sky.

What do people think, when out
of the corner of their eye they catch
my softly glowing star and discover
this lightly shining object, though
almost gone and wonder what it is.

To answer, I'd have to say, It's me!
But why would I decide to write a poem
about a lonely star, lost in trillions of
others in a rarely searched nighttime sky?

The title is *I'm a Lonely Star* because
I'm the lonely person caught in the middle
of a worldwide, mortal pandemic with
people dying in record numbers.

The words *highly contagious* have reached a new
meaning. I understand the Coronavirus is ten times
more contagious than germs of other flus. Micro-
organisms are spread by close proximity and coughing.

Best avoidance is wearing a mask and
maintaining six feet of social distancing.
All concert halls, auditoriums, stadiums,
schools, restaurants, parties and places
of close indoor circulation are banned.

Perhaps if I really were a lonely star lost in
the magnitude of some great cosmos and far from
the possibility of contamination, I'd be better
able to delight in omnipresent miracles.

Commercial – From Prose

A young architect is completing his house
and showing it off to his fiancée, or wife,
or girlfriend. And as they make their rounds,
his brilliance and profundity of the architect's

design becomes overwhelming. They laugh
and joke until that appropriate moment
(the point of the film), when they smile,
gaze into each other's eyes and take up a

can of Pepsi for a toast. *"To the most wonderful
elixir in the world, Pepsi-Cola."* I thought
the part of the male lead was not yet cast.
The director seemed to be looking over the

heads of everyone for someone to play the
architect. I extended myself to my full height,
five-feet seven inches, casually crossed my
legs, folded my arms and leaned significantly

against a doorjamb with a straight face.
Within his full view I assumed the pose of
what I thought was the gifted architect look.
The director caught my eye, looked me up

and down and then lost himself among
the workmen. He came back with a boyish-
looking young man about five foot ten,
athletic, and dressed in clean Saturday

clothes. His skin golden brown from the
sun and with a shock of hair carelessly
slanting over one eye, he wore an open-
necked sports shirt with brown slacks and

leather boots. As comedian Bob Newhart says,
"He had a crooked smile, but straight teeth."
As it turns out the actor actually was a licensed
architect from Long Beach and had been

selected to play the lead alongside a cute,
smiling, prom queen-type young lady.
They performed successfully, I guess, but
what did I know? As the song goes,

"I tried, but I couldn't do it. I tried,
but I couldn't do it. I tried..." I think I saw
the commercial later, or may have heard
from friends that it had aired back east.

Pink City - On Abstract Art

In abstract art,
the rules of the game
are to loosen the sails
of our imagination
and explore the wind,
the weather and
distant shores.

        The meaning of this
        artwork must be invented!

I see a land of color and fun
the likes of which I've never known.

        A shocking pink sky
        is a background
        for burning red,
        the underpinning
        of black and blue
        supporting a comic city.

The tiny town forms
an eccentric home
for miniature people
dressed in outlandish
costumes, scurrying
this way and that
in their funny homeland
on scooters or roller skates

doing their business,
managing, directing or
laughing away their lives.

How long will they exist?
Are they permanent folks
built for a lifetime,
or will they live in
the shred of a mind
of a single mortal?

Will they outlive us,
or are these permanent
persons built for the life
and length of the cosmos?

Will they be gone tomorrow?
Or are they seen like a fleeting
glimpse through the dusty
window of a passing bus?

Were they conceived
at this special moment
at this particular time
in this exacting instance
never to return, or should
I go home with my foolishness
and have a cup of tea?

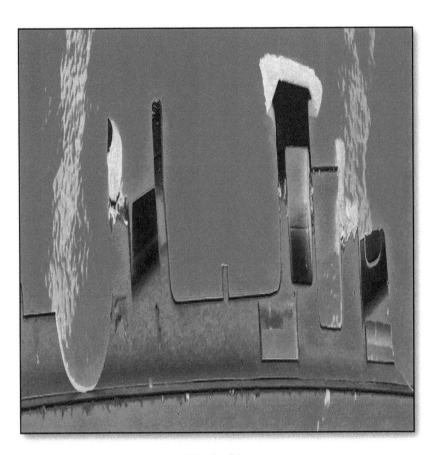

Pink City

I Am a Tree - Poetry

I am a tree!

Not again!
No! No! No! **I am a tree!**

You're taken with yourself.
"Figuratively speaking" I'm a tree.

What are you "normally" speaking?
OK! Sometimes I *feel* like I'm a tree.

How does a tree feel?
I don't know how a tree feels!
What I said has nothing to do
with *how* a tree feels! I said,
"figuratively speaking," thank you.
I am a tree, meaning I feel like what
I think the inner spirit, soul and
body, of a tree feels about itself.
I'm talking as if I knew, which I don't.
This is a poem about *feelings.*

Why didn't you say sometimes
you feel like a tree? Is it
a big tree or a little tree?

A big tree! OK! Sometimes I feel
like my roots are buried deep
in the ground spreading from
my trunk where it unites with

the ground in a great round ball. Sort
of grabbing the earth with the compelling
force of ten monstrous giants.

You don't say!
My trunk, once free of the earth,
plunges upward into the air from the
power of my root system with the
strength of mighty oaks to reach its
slender tip moving gently in the breeze.

Cool, man!
The wide expanse of leaves and branches
have been touched by nature's magic and
in the early fall have turned a brilliant
yellow with traces of green, orange and
red. The steady breeze rattles the leaves
showing the leaf's upper-side green at
times and the lower-side yellow. The steady
sound of the wind hums a whispering tone
in anticipation of fall and coming winter.

That's how you feel?
That's why you say,
I am a tree?

I have to look at the tree and feel
the wind and relish the colors and
while in the throes, ***I am a tree!***
Hot damn!

Rick as a Brother – **From Prose**
After a while I came to like some of Rick's
poems and when I received another,
whether I understood it or not, I took
it as a complement. I was flattered he

> considered me worthy enough to
> copy a poem, address an envelope,
> stamp it and mail it. Through his
> poetry he shared his deepest feelings.

I decided it was good to be worthy
enough to receive another's
deepest feelings. Eventually
I began to like Rick because he

> thought about life and trusted me.
> I would not belittle his poetic efforts.
> I was honorable enough for his
> deepest sharing. Before love there

is *trust. We trusted each other.*
Later I came to love Rick like
a brother. Perhaps he appreciated
me because I helped him get the

> *Gilman-Young job, though I don't*
> *think the state of architecture was*
> *his first concern. He stayed with*
> *Gilman-Young for two years until*

work got slow and then accepted a
position helping the USC Marine Biology
Department do oceanographic studies
on a floating island of the arctic ice in Alaska.

Circles - On Abstract Art

With whirls, abandon and
borders, the circles are insane.

See the recklessness!

Who can stop passion so intense
and irrational as to be mortally
injured by a persisting process?

Like turning the spigot to
high not realizing the limits!

Why is it spinning? Combining
the color of red with the happiness
of orange is like forming a symbol
of strength and endurance with fortitude!

Why do circles go crazy
on a background of blue?

The whirls are bizarre and
so out of touch they've
torn formidable black into
tatters and shreds and passionate
red into fire and blood.

Though I have to admit
while senselessness and
passion are brought to dizzying
chaos, it has not yet exploded.

Shrieks and bubbles of
Yellow, while crazily spinning,
are amazingly alive.

Through turmoil and trouble,
they make a powerful strength.

The perfect picture
OF DESTRUCTION?

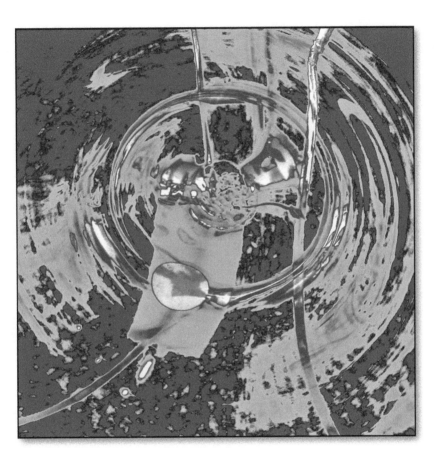

Circles

Bothering that I See? - Poetry

Inner agitation.

What agitation?

Agitation is hard to define.

Try!

A feeling of unpleasantness.

What unpleasantness?

Advanced age.

How long?

Perhaps a year or more.

What else?

The state of humanity.

The pandemic that's worldwide
preventing social contact
by closing schools, stadiums,
theaters, concerts, malls
and public gatherings.
In a larger sense,
for the whole world
a total loss of socialization!

Global warming dismays me;
the destruction of Earth as I know it.
The total obliteration of the world I see
as the miracle of our only heaven.

My despondency over the
inability of our species
to maintain the last,
finishing, ultimate,

concluding and final place in the
cosmos for all that's living to live.
Why do you feel this so strongly?
Doesn't everybody? I never
thought this would happen.
  You are agitated because you
  have empathy for the planet?
It's something to which I never gave credence.
Something so impossible, it never entered my mind.
Something so final and so permanent
causing suffering and death to all living species
  Plants, fish, insects, birds
  and bees are diminishing.
  Monarch butterflies are disappearing.
  The freshwater table is dangerously low.
  Ocean levels are rising.
  Barrier reefs and the bottom
   of the food chain are shrinking.
Wildfires are advancing.
Summers are too hot.
Humans increase exponentially.
Symptoms are strongly evident.
The prognosis is devastating
  and *unchangeable.*
That's what's bothering me.

Groundbreaking Ceremony – From Prose

Roy was standing next to the last of the
Triggers with reins in hand displaying
Hollywood charisma. He wore a white

> Stetson hat, white shirt with fancy
> red embroidery, hip-hugging white
> Levi's and natural leather boots.
> Dale stood nearby apparently

talking with officials and was
wearing white riding pants,
white boots, a white sombrero,
a small red bandana and a

> leather jacket fringed with
> bouncing natural leather strings.
> She looked like a hoedown
> singer between acts. Roy and

Dale brightened the place like
neon lights. They were glowing
human showpieces and claimed
absolute attention from those

> who appeared to be developers,
> financiers and real estate moguls.
> Two or three photographers
> selected ever-changing positions

and snapped numerous pictures
from every angle. The ritual
of groundbreaking was short.
In fact, I don't even remember it.

Perhaps I didn't stay for it.
There was talk of food,
but I didn't see any.
I don't think I shook hands,

certainly not with Roy.
Though I was the only
architect whose work
for which they were

      breaking ground, and the
      single architect whose
      efforts were to set an example
      for a multimillion-dollar

development establishing
another beginning for none
other than the Russcor
Development Company,

      a subsidiary of the giant
      American Hawaiian Land
      Company, as well as movie
      stars Roy Rogers and Dale Evans,

I came away feeling unnoticed.
Was there a lesson in this?
Was I disillusioned?
Was I becoming mature?

A Rainy Day - On Abstract Art.

A rainy day is a complex piece of work.
Black at the bottom; a serious presence.

Intrusions of white are symbolic
of ideas meant to convey.

Crosshatchings in blue are the message.
Matching shadows the reinforcement

from the unknown above.
Green and black drippings
suggest inclement weather.

Is this left-brain picture analyzed
by right-brain thought?

Do we trust the left brain
for intimate right-brain feelings?

If the answer is feelings,
the question is what are they?

Since I did the artwork,
only I would know.
I don't, but it might be

"Ruminations on a rainy day."

A Rainy Day

Look to the left and See! - Poetry
The sun is sinking.

Where does it go?
Through blackened trees,
then beneath the world.

How many have you seen?
"Let Me Count the Days."
92 x 365 = 33,945. In two weeks,
I'll have seen 34 thousand days.

Let us think, then,
behind black trees
the sun, in fading light
for this day only
moving forever,
taking its time,
neither too fast
nor too slow,
where does it go?
It drops down in the west!
Under the ocean!
Then up in China!
To visit Europe,
and then the Atlantic,
before reaching New York.

Then, three more hours
until it lightens our day.

The sun descending
a verified principle,
the undeniable fact,
the indisputable certainty
and irrefutable truth.
Today is over!

Rain – From Prose

It rained straight for nine days and
ten nights with no letup. It didn't
rain lightly, but came either strong
or in torrents. It beat against our

      windows and trailed in streams off
      our eaves and decks to form erosive
      channels on the hillside leading to
      wider tributaries. With wind driving
      the rain uphill, we were drenched from

below as well as from above. The one
thing it did do was rain continuously,
all day, all night, moment-to-moment,
hour-to-hour, for nine long days. The
media called it the Pineapple Express,

      a continuous flow of rain-laden clouds
      blowing across the Pacific from the
      direction of Hawaii and dropping moisture
      to give Southern California a complete
      soaking. We were getting a rain test!

To quote from my usual reference
book for 1969, *"Rains in California
caused mudslides that destroyed
or damaged 10,000 homes and
killed 100."* It was gloomy. It was

hard to work. It dampened spirits.
The canyons were closed. We couldn't
drive. Construction stopped. During the
first three days the ground became
saturated and Malibu Creek thickened

and began its heavy flow, rumbling
toward the ocean. On the third day,
up and down the coast, I saw swirls of
sediment-laden water curled in brown,
dirty hoops a quarter-mile offshore.

The ocean looked invaded, worried and
unhappy with itself. While trying to sleep
on the sixth night, Karon and I were
disconcerted when we heard an unfamiliar
throaty roar rising from Malibu Creek.

The eerie sound penetrated the whole
estuary and was caused by huge boulders
one to four feet in diameter on their
forced trip downstream clacking and
grunting over one another. This continued

each night and for the remainder of the rain.
The sandy strip that usually separated the
lagoon from the ocean had long since been
penetrated and a wide, dirty stream of river-
water had forced its way through the barrier,
invading the ocean. Everyone was distraught!

Shape Like Flower - On Abstract Art

The shape like a flower rises from a clear vase.
It contains four colors: green, blue, yellow and gray.
The stick figure in the center I call *"the brain,"* and
it appears as a gentle little man swimming in the
happiness of his own lines and dots, meaning he's
joyful and delighted in the value of his creation.

> Green and growth symbolize his own
> soul. Blue is purity. Whitish-yellow is
> intelligence. At the top, tiny buds of
> gray and green dance under a pure sky,
> ready at any time to burst into being.

I made this picture over 50 years ago. I've
always called it one of my *no-think* drawings.
Long ago, when I got up in the morning, I
wanted to do an artwork with paper and oil-
pastels. I needed to draw, but had no idea what.

> But that was good! Because my intent was
> to tap into my subconscious mind to find
> out what was in there, and drawing without
> knowing what, was easier than planning
> what to draw. Of course I found out later
> the unconscious mind is not about logic such
> as reading books or doing mathematics.

Drawings without thought point to a more
general nature called *feelings*. This was something
I hadn't thought of before. _Shape Like a Flower_ was
composed with blue, green and gray lines and dots
finished at the top with even more gray dots. If the
drawing were about feelings, what were they?

> The green stick shape in the center appears as
> a logical, straight-thinking individual; a lively
> little man dancing in the center of his own art.
> After doing 155 of these no-think drawings, I
> found the center of the artwork is the *"brain"* of
> the piece; the key to further growth, or meaning.

The portion surrounding the brain embellishes and
finalizes the meaning of the *"brain."* It details the
message and the overall awareness of the unconscious
mind that *dominates the person at this point in time.*

> The unconscious mind contains the auto-
> biographical self with all its memories, hopes, fears
> and everything pertaining to its personal
> life including what happened yesterday,
> and fears and joys about tomorrow.

I know this is helpful, but may not know why.

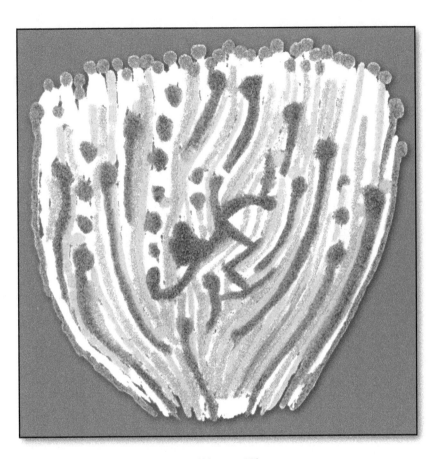

Shape like a Flower

Look Up and See - Poetry
Natural wood with grain and knots!

Of what are you reminded?
A person in shadow who is not me,
but the foundation of who I am.

How so?
He's stupid, uninformed,
and has no ideas.
He's unenlightened
and at the mercy of life
with all its dealings,
but his questions are cool.
He's forthright and honest
and wishes no harm,
but charming in a way
and earnest for answers.

How so?
Were I tempted to steal a waitress's
tip, he'd ask with too-open eyes
in a too-candid voice,

"Are you honest or dishonest?"
Suddenly aware
of so direct a question,
I'm forced to divulge
the ultimate response to
"am I honest or dishonest?"

I choose what my mother taught,
to remain honest.

For honest is life
and dishonest is death.

Chief Harvey Anderson – From Prose

About twelve noon, just beyond the town
of Pearblossom, I was getting hungry.
Harvey spied a fruit stand on a hot
narrow highway and swerved across

> the street to stop in a dusty parking
> lot next to a canvas-covered wooden
> shack selling fruit and vegetables.
> Mixed with corn, tomatoes, plums,

strawberries and other organic foods
were round firm tree-ripe cling
peaches. Harvey enthusiastically
bought a dozen, and then pulling

> back on the highway and picking
> up speed, he began reaching into
> the bag and eating while driving.
> Wind bustling in through the open

window, he held out a peach and
asked me to eat as many as I wanted.
With one hand traveling at 80 miles
an hour Harvey took huge bites of

> the delicious fruit. Juice occasionally
> dripped from his chin and with the
> back of his hand he'd wipe his face
> before taking another enormous bite.

Halfway through the peach he'd
spit the seed out the window,
swallow the other half in two bites,
and reach for another. We were

> having tree-ripened peaches for lunch!
> They were so juicy they served as both
> food and drink. While he chewed he
> talked about how good and rich and

nurturing and thirst-quenching the
peaches were. He bragged about
how much he loved them and
ravenously ate several again spitting

> the seeds out the window and wiping
> his hands with a handkerchief. We
> had a companionable time driving
> along the narrow desert highways

and shouting to be heard over the hot
wind blowing in our ears. We continued
to Victorville, then back to Apple Valley
and Hesperia. At five-thirty in the

> afternoon, we drove to a tired stop
> at Malibu Fire Station. I loved my trip
> with the Chief. I learned a lot about
> the Fire Chief business and the trip

gave me a better opportunity
to know ***Chief Harvey Anderson.***

Aflame with Desire - On Abstract Art

With a release of compulsive

    destruction the red

flame is burning something down!

    The blistering purple background

in all its fame and glory

    aggravates the flame.

The hot, burning, flaming fire

    whips towards the sky

obliterating everything in which

    it contacts and is impossible

to stop. With drive and provocation

    the imposing dark blue unit

in the lower left hand corner

    could be the symbol

of Corporate America

about to burst into flame.

Are we now to believe

Corporate America

is about to go up in flames?

We recovered against Germany

and Japan, as well, by removing cities

Nagasaki and Hiroshima,

and as I study this picture

despite the beauty of its colors,

I'm disappointed for mankind.

There has been an absence

of compassion and nobility.

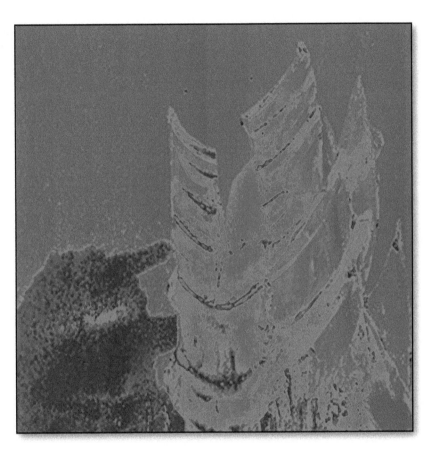

Aflame with Desire

Look Down and See - Poetry

A grain of sand
dense as wind.

    A hole in wood.
    Dirt in a hole in wood.
    Brown gash and a hole in wood.
    Visualize a comet through grain

going somewhere
through night sky
to an unknown place
never to be found,
like a lost memory,
or the eternity of
unawakened sleep.

    'Til that fateful day
    when through rays of light
    a dragon appeared
    and announced
    that the time had come
    to be the witness
    of a long lost secret.

Only to be told
on a special day,
a male in full glory
sprang from the void
and traveled at breakneck

speed over the wilds,
over the water,
over the mountains
to seek a mate.

And after waiting
for endless moments
to meet a love
and conceive another
out of nothingness
into this world
of joy,
of sorrow,
of happiness
and endless days
he decided to bring forth

Another life!

Eyes – From Prose

I remember a tough looking young man
who came to our discussion group named
Dave Fagel. In faded jeans and blue work
shirt, Dave was a wiry, 29-year-old Synanon
member with prematurely graying black hair.

> *(Synanon was a private self-help foundation
> for drug addicts.)* For any Synanon member
> to leave the building on Ocean Avenue in
> Santa Monica was considered a temptation to
> drug use, but Dave had special permission
> to visit. One spring evening before our

discussion group debate, Dave Fagel and I
were having a one-to-one conversation standing
on our concrete terrace overlooking Santa
Monica Canyon. The fragrance of spring flowers
filled the late-evening air and the lower, darker

> continuation of the sky blending into black at
> the foot of the canyon was the ocean. I don't
> remember what we were talking about, but
> Dave told me, not with words, but with a grin
> on his young and weathered face, that he'd

conquered things of which I couldn't even
dream. He looked compellingly up to me
and I saw directly into the light in his blue eyes.
They were spiritual, open and accepting.
They held the optimism of a sunny ocean

on a breezy day. I blinked once or twice with
embarrassment and understood his wordless
message. His eyes told me of his acceptance
of me and if I were willing, my acceptance of
him. His eyes told me we were special creatures

on this miraculous earth and that we had a
right to enjoy our unique existence together.
I won't forget those eyes, so clean, so clear,
so open and so true. His clear blue eyes

were willing to be looked in to and willing to
look into mine. It was as if he were allowing
me to enter his soul and by so doing we could
enter all souls. At once, my soul joined his.

New Thought - On Abstract Art

Fiery red heat glows
behind dark blue shapes
that speak of dusk and sky.

Thoughts of lapis lazuli arise
as outlandish footprints of
some giant night creature
enigmatically reappear.

Blue is an element unmoved
by hot green colors, but
inspired by heat and the
predominance of soul.

Soul is the light of the world;
a willingness comparable
to *"the birth of a child,"*
or the *"durability of death,"*
or an emerging passion, as
prevalent as the *"missing link."*

With no argument, red
confirms the words, *"I care!"*

Can the blue of soul exist
while overcoming the universal
heat of passionate red?
Green is a willingness to grow
and shall not be refused!

When the immovable force
meets the invincible object the
invisible answer cements the two.

Fiery-hot blue and
green-growing health
become *"the whole."*

The whole begins
at the *"Big Bang"*
with stars so real as
they rush away and
eventually install

the Milky Way with nine
fine planets containing
oceans, mountains, tsunamis,
tornados and too many humans.

Then a land I have never seen,

"the quantum world"
where waves of light collapse
leaving just a particle,
and scientists pull their hair

and ask, *"Why? Why? Why?"*
And over time, you can bet
what's left is still another *"Why?"*

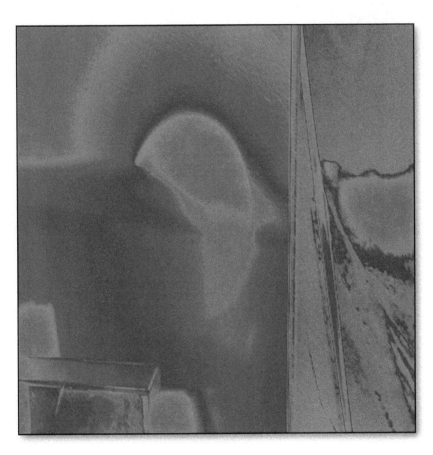

New Thought

I Am the Wind - Poetry

I am the wind.

> *No, you're not!*

Yeah! I am the wind!

> *You look like my buddy.*

I don't mean I move eerily
through an old, dark house
snuffing out the last candle. I mean
"figuratively speaking" I'm a candle!
I mean I am the wind. Sorry!

> *Jesus Christ! Get it together.*
> *Are you the wind or a candle?*

I dreamed I am the wind!
"Figuratively speaking," that is.

> *Well, I'm glad that's over.*
> *See you tomorrow!*

Wait! Don't you want to know
why I dreamed I'm the wind?

> *Naw! I'm in a rush! I've got to*
> *see a mouse about some cheese.*

Suddenly, awakened in the middle of
the night, from high above I heard a roar
howling and crying through the trees. The
power of a new storm was unable to be stopped.

> *Yeah! Well, I gotta go.*

The gale was formidable, unyielding and
moved with the resolution of life or death.

Let me know how that works out.
Don't you have a smidgeon of curiosity?

How long would it take you to spell it out?
A fraction of a second.

OK! Hit me with the fraction!
The wind persisted through the night.
In the early morning light, it continued
to whip and flow through acres of
wheat fields, now bent by a gale that
pounded across the plains. Quickly,
it came to the edge of a pond leaping
and thrashing through waves blown
to a frenzy. Thereafter, the unrelenting
wind moved swiftly into the forest.

Hey! That's pretty cool!
See you later.
Don't you want to know
why I had the dream?

OK! Why did you have the dream?
I was hoping you'd tell me.

I'm not clairvoyant!
We'll never know?

Guess not. Goodbye!

Trip to Tucson – From Prose

At 22 years old, I had 8 months' experience
in an authentic architectural office of
which I was not particularly proud.
I had finished Denver skiing, swimming,
golfing and dating and run out of enthusiasm
      for the piano. I asked about other jobs,
      but couldn't find the passion to make
      a real try. There was one successful
      architect in Denver, William Muchow,
      who graduated ten years or so earlier
      than I from the University of Illinois.
He headed his large firm and it was said
he did good contemporary work. Drafting
in his office with intelligent supervision
might have been a possibility. But, I didn't
      pursue it and didn't analyze myself
      about it. I probably thought he wouldn't
      have hired me anyway, or I was afraid
      of failure if I were to work in a good
      office. My youthful spirit was calling me
away from Denver and to the southwest.
News came from Chicago that brother,
Dave, not only had become the President
of his high school senior class, but had also
won a football scholarship to the University
      of Arizona at Tucson. Suddenly the lust
      for new adventure invaded my soul. I
      would drive my new 13-year-old Chevy
      across country and visit Dave in Tucson
      as I wandered aimlessly toward California.

I gave my two-weeks' notice, offered
thanks to Chuck Hazlewood and the
guys in the office, expressed my
appreciation for the help and hospitality
to the Shutners, and on October 3,
       1950, drove off in my 1937 Chevy
       with $200.00 in my pocket calculated
       only to last as long as it would. I left it
       to faith when the money was gone I'd
       find another job. The $200.00 would
at least get me to Tucson. My plans were
not definite. I wasn't conscious of it, but
in those days I was searching for myself.
I wouldn't know who I was until I found me.
I was a guy not through with sports, not
       through with adolescence, partially age-
       appropriate, afraid of life, anxious to do
       the right thing for my future, full of promise,
       shy, yet equipped with most of the right
       stuff. I was everything and nothing –
an assembly of contradictions and loaded
with promise and hope for a good future.
I was doing the next thing, a healthy, educated
pawn of feelings and fate, going on guts
and desire, hoping to get lucky. I was anxious
       about failure while being afraid of
       success and desirous of a long
       delayed female relationship.

Tornado – On Abstract Art

Pink and purple rages across
space as if from the silent
breath of the outer cosmos.

       I'm taken by its royal color
       and its flagrant energy and
       am swept into thoughts of
       the cryptic and unknown.

There's a black tornado
that seems to have sprung
into existence by the
mysterious rudiments
of the pink and purple.

       It rises off a slim black line
       that must have been its origin
       and tangles with the lofty space
       of the upper atmosphere.

It's so exemplary of something
cosmic, how can this not be
something archetypal? I cannot
help being reminded of outer
space and Universal Time.

       Some say time doesn't exist
       and we count time by how long
       it takes to get from one piece
       of matter to the next.

Some say matter exists
and time does not.
Time is not matter
and matter is not time.

> We have two entities that will
> never be anything else. They
> are stuck in relation to them-
> selves and change will be never.

The best we can do with
how long it takes to get from
one piece of matter to the next
is to make good use of time.

> Where does this leave tornadoes?
> High in an atmosphere ruled only
> by time and space using time astutely
> and moving with unrivalled greatness.

Tornado

Dream Poem with Bicycle - Dream

It's gray.
It's getting dark.
It's late twilight.
It's the time just
before black night.

　　　It's imperative in
　　　a too distant town
　　　I attend a meeting.

A friend will lend
me transportation;
a car or motorcycle.

　　　Approaching the highway
　　　wearing a long-sleeved T-shirt
　　　I'm dressed too light
　　　and am already cold.

It's a bicycle!

　　　I haven't the address.
　　　I'm not even warm.
　　　My destination's unclear.
　　　It's time to leave.

To be pumping a bicycle,
the distance is too far
when I'm cold.
so far in the night.

"Going so far on a bicycle
at night when I'm cold in the
dark and not knowing where"
is the meaning of the dream.

I wake.

Foggy Day - From Prose

When I went out wisps of cottony fog drifted
in masses over the estuary to evaporate somewhere inland. For every vaporous mass that
enveloped the beach and vanished, another
quickly took its place, only to vanish once again.

> Sometimes the sun would appear full strength
> and I could see my board, the clear, smooth
> water and catch a glimpse of the pier before
> it was again lost from view. In the shadow
> of the intermittent fog, the ocean was thick
> and black, a molten glass deeply breathing.

The ocean gently lifted me before taking its
comfortable time to quietly hiss as it gently
collapsed against the shore. Immensely enjoying
the cool air against my skin and my cooler legs
dangling in the water, I prone-paddled farther out
fantasizing I'd meet a radical set of waves moving

> resolutely in the open seas from Hawaii. I'd
> hang a right, run to the nose and ride the tube
> to the sand. But as I moved outward a cooler
> wind darkened my board as well as my spirits
> and my impermanent view of the shore was
> even further obscured.

Only now and then could I see a suggestion
of the beach, until an even larger mass of fog
swept suddenly off the colder ocean and I found

myself enveloped in thick fog. The sun
was gone. I could no longer see the beach
and couldn't hear the breaking waves. It
was very much darker and I thought, *perhaps*
this was not a good surfing day after all.

> I made motions to paddle in, then stopped.
> Which way was the shore? I couldn't hear
> the surf or see the pier or mountains.
> The swells moved up, then down with no
> sound or suggestion of direction. Everything
> was cold, gray, windy, dark and ominous.

As my imagination frequently allows me to do,
I leapt to the worst-case scenario. Swallowing
panic I asked myself, *could this be a permanent*
fog? Would I be out all night? Suddenly, I was
cold and hungry! I needed to go to the bathroom.
Which way should I paddle? I didn't expect this!
I want to be in my warm living room watching TV.

> After fifteen minutes of agonized waiting,
> the heavier fog slowly dematerialized. The
> atmosphere lightened and I caught just the
> merest suggestion of the beach. My heart
> leaped and I paddled furiously. I thought
> luck has saved me from a watery death.

I imagined I probably would have been
found the next morning floating a few hundred
yards past the pelican raft, exhausted, freezing,
hungry, shivering and hugging my board.

Sacred Site - On Abstract Art

I'm struggling to make sense of the
number of messages I'm getting from
this picture. To examine colors first,
there's a predominance of blue and

black augmented by several unrecognizable
shapes of orange with wisps of purple
drifting throughout. From a color standpoint,
I must be satisfied that dark blue equals

depth and stability, black gives us power
and authority, not to be diminished
by orange representing happiness and
enthusiasm. With wispy purple as a tint, the

whole picture reflects royalty.
From a color standpoint only, the
picture has the basic message of depth,
power, mystery and extravagance.

The center of interest is a word in
bluish-white, seemingly written
in Asian or Japanese surrounded by
an excess of things I've explained before.

If the said inscription were a word, its
meaning would be vital and we'd know the
picture's purpose. If not, the so-called
Asian word is still the center of interest

telling the viewer all that must be conveyed.
Other than the top-to-bottom almost
vertical shape at the right, the remaining
portions of the picture are angular triangles

and trapezoids tending to stabilize one
another. And so what is the meaning of
the picture? It's an elaborate and
rather powerful representation of a

written symbol denoting something
enormous, important, joyful and non-
threatening, such as the meaning of life and
death, of which everyone should be aware.

Sacred Site

I Am the Rain - Poetry

I am the rain!

No shit?
NO! I am the Rain!

You don't look like the rain.
Yeah? What do I look like?

You look like shit!
Aren't you being a little hard on me?

Yeah! I guess so.
What do you mean,
"I am the rain?"
OK! Maybe I'm not the rain,
but the air has a yellow cast
and very still and in the distance
it looks like it's clouding up.
There's a quiet hush before
the storm and a sense that
something deep inside me
will break upon the world
and attack the earth with a
resounding crash and just
for a moment turn everything
into light, before everything's dark.

I can get that!
I've had that feeling.
No shit!

You're starting to sound like me.
I am you!

What do you mean I am you?
We're the same person.

You're kidding!
How do you know?
We're both talking to us.
Look in the mirror.
What do you see?

My face!
I hate to tell you this,
but the face you see is mine.

No shit!
If you don't believe me
ask the person in the mirror

Are you ME?
Yes, I'm you!

No shit! Is this some kind of trick?
At times, one person can be two people.

I thought you were the rain!
That's crazy as shit!

Johnny Fain, Sr. – From Prose

The lower floor was a store leased to
Johnny Fain, Sr., who sold and repaired
television sets. Johnny Fain Sr., the father
of renowned surfboard rider Johnny Fain Jr.

> was short, skinny and tough.
> In his mid-40s, he told me he'd
> been a stand-in for the 1940s
> tough-guy actor, Brian Donlevy.

Since he'd also been a boxer, he
did all of Donlevy's fight scenes.
From time to time I'd talk to
Johnny Sr. and we soon became

> friendly acquaintances. Johnny
> was well known throughout
> Malibu, especially at a restaurant
> called The Cottage and the

Paradise Cove Bar. He never
told me this, nor do I know
who told it to me, but I
understand when he'd had

> too much to drink he sometimes
> had difficulty controlling his temper.
> Toward the end of an evening of
> drinking, if he thought someone

had insulted him, he'd invite him
outside, whatever his opponent's size,
to settle it in the parking lot. There,
he'd kick the holy bejesus out of him.

      I didn't go to the Cottage or
      Paradise Cove Bar, so I don't
      know if there's any truth to it,
      but it makes a good story.

Johnny never drank on the
job as far as I could tell and I,
being aware of his personality,
was careful in my conversations.

      I didn't want to tick Johnny off and
      have to settle it on the Coast Highway.

END

Other Books by Doug Rucker

Personal Journey
Poems predicting next phase of life

Early Stories
Autobiography - Birth through University

Groundwork
Autobiography - Marriage to office opening

Growing Edge
Autobiography – Office to house burning

Moving Through
Collection of poems with *"No Think"* pastels

Book of Words
Essay collection - Humor & philosophy

Harold and the Acid Sea of Reality
My thoughts on fantasy & reality

Trial by Fire – A Tale of two Houses
Burning and rebuilding of home

Building a Home that Loves You
A Post-and-Beam Architectural Philosophy

Thinking in the Abstract
The meaning of abstract art

About the Author

Born in Elmhurst Illinois, a suburb of Chicago, Doug attended the University of Illinois in Champaign-Urbana and graduated with a bachelor of science in architecture. In 1955, he built his first house in Santa Monica Canyon, California, and in the following years his wife gave birth to three marvelous daughters. By January of 1958, he became the first permanent architect doing business solely in Malibu. In 1966, he moved his family into a new Malibu architect's dream home overlooking Surfrider Beach. Five years later, it burned to the ground and it took him two more years to build a more fire-resistant house over the same foundations. The new house remains noted in *Gebhardt and Winter's Los Angeles Guide to Architecture*. Doug has spent most of his career doing new houses and additions in Malibu and local areas, but has also designed and built single jobs in Kauai, Greece, Denver, Fallbrook, Barstow and Long Beach as well as eight projects in Santa Barbara. In 1980, he was divorced from his first wife and for 43 years was married to Marge Lewi-Rucker who had four children of her own. All are grown and passionately invested in their own lives.

Marge has since passed, and Doug now lives content in the mountains above Malibu on a landscaped acre of property in a house of his own design. Retired from architecture, he brings a special passion to writing and photographic digital art.